Trusting God
In Troubling Times

A Daily Devotional

Trusting God
In Troubling Times

A Daily Devotional

Trusting God In Troubling Times

Copyright © 2025 by Dr. Jamie T. Pleasant; Ph.D.

Biblion Publishing LLC

All rights reserved. No portion of this book may be reproduced, stored in a retrieval system or transmitted in any form or by any means — electronic, mechanical, photocopy, recording or other without the prior written authorization of the author — except for a brief quotation in printed reviews. Unless otherwise indicated, scripture quotations are taken from the Holy Bible, especially, the New International Version, King James Version and English Standard Version.

First Edition / First Printing

Getting the most out of

"Trusting God In Troubling Times"

Are you ready to increase your trust level? Do you want to walk in the peace and confidence that God has planned for you? Do you need a daily guide and reading plan to get you to a new place of trusting Him? If you answered yes to any of these questions, this devotional is for you! *"Trusting God In Troubling Times"* will take you on a journey to realize the blessings that God has ordained for you to walk in right now! Each day presents a Scripture reference and personal message, a focused prayer, a plan of action, and reflections for each reading. *"Trusting God In Troubling Times"* will help you reach a new level of divine trust in a trustworthy God! You will learn new ways to stay motivated and inspired. You will walk in a newness of joy, peace, contentment, abundance, and prosperity as you complete each daily guide and reading plan in this devotional. Get ready to be blessed beyond what you can think or imagine, as you begin to possess a new level of trust that will go beyond your understanding and straight into your heart!

Dedication

To my daddy, Anthony T. Pleasant, who was a perfect example to me of what a man should be. I miss you so much and love you with all of my heart!

To my mother, Bertha Pleasant; you loved me so much and laid the foundation for my financial success! I can't wait to see you again!

To my pulchritudinous wife Kimberly, and my children Christian, Zion, and Nacara.

To the New Zion Christian Church Family. You are a true blessing in my life!

Humbly Yours in Christ,

Apostle Jamie T. Pleasant

Trusting God In Troubling Times

Trusting God In Troubling Times Devotional Synopsis

Congratulations on purchasing this devotional! Get ready to achieve a new level of trust through your daily reading through this devotional. This devotional is filled with scriptures, prayers, and commentaries that God Yahweh personally spoke to me to share with you. This devotional will guide you into a deeper revelation of God's plan for increasing your level of trust in Him to be able to live a triumphant life— beginning now! Some ending prayer sections will have the acronym "IJNA" which means In Jesus' name, amen.

Devotion Topic Page Guide

Devotion Theme	Pages
General help with trust	14, 18, 22, 126
Doubt in our government	30, 34, 186, 190, 194, 198
Need for racial equality	50, 54, 58, 62
Fear of losing necessities	38, 42, 118, 122, 138
Lack of peace	82, 86, 98
Fear of losing material things	26, 46, 138
Fear of losing wealth	66, 70, 74
Overcoming anxiety	90, 94
Dealing with difficult times	114, 134
Employment challenges	102, 106, 110
Ignoring negative thoughts	178, 182
Getting a good night's sleep	166, 170, 174
Comfort during bereavement	142, 146, 150
In need of healing	154, 158, 162
God's plan & protection	78, 130

Trusting God In Troubling Times

^{23} **Buy truth, and do not sell it; buy wisdom, instruction, and understanding.**

Proverbs 23:23 (ESV)

Trusting God In Troubling Times

Trusting God In Troubling Times

Trusting God In Troubling Times

Day One

> Trust in the Lord with all your heart, and do not lean on your own understanding. (Proverbs 3:5, ESV)

Trusting God means that you must learn to accept how He does things. You must never forget that He doesn't have to give you details. He only needs to tell you that He has it all under control.

Focused Prayer

God Yahweh, help me to trust you in these troubling times that I am facing. I need your comfort and assurance that can only come from you touching my heart with your assuring words. In Jesus' name, Amen.

My Action Plan

_____

_____

_____

_____

_____

_____

_____

Trusting God In Troubling Times

Personal Blessings I Have Experienced

Trusting God In Troubling Times

Personal Reflection

and

Final Thoughts

Day Two

> Commit your way to the Lord; trust in him, and he will act. (Psalm 37:5, ESV)

Trusting God Yahweh means that you must give up expecting Him to conform to your plans. You must now let Him shape your plans and provide the path that He wants you to take.

Focused Prayer

God Yahweh, I surrender my ways to you. I have tried it on my own and have run into many obstacles. I now place my life under your direction. Lead me in the right way to be blessed eternally by you. In Jesus' name, Amen.

My Action Plan

_____

_____

_____

_____

_____

_____

_____

Trusting God In Troubling Times

Personal Blessings I Have Experienced

Trusting God In Troubling Times

Personal Reflection

and

Final Thoughts

_____

_____

_____

_____

_____

_____

_____

_____

_____

_____

_____

_____

Day Three

> The Lord is my strength and my shield; in him my heart trusts, and I am helped; my heart exults, and with my song I give thanks to him.
> (Psalm 28:7, ESV)

Trusting God Yahweh means that you must do more than say that you trust Him. You must prove that you trust Him by knowing in your heart that He is going to help and strengthen you during tough times.

Focused Prayer

God Yahweh, Please send a sign to me in my heart that you are going to take care of what I am dealing with right now. I love you, and I want my trust to match my love for you. I need you to strengthen my heart to totally trust what I cannot see. In Jesus' name, Amen.

My Action Plan

_____

_____

_____

_____

_____

_____

_____

_____

Trusting God In Troubling Times

_____

_____

_____

_____

_____

Personal Blessings I Have Experienced

_____

_____

_____

_____

_____

_____

_____

_____

Trusting God In Troubling Times

Personal Reflection

and

Final Thoughts

_____

_____

_____

_____

_____

_____

_____

_____

_____

_____

_____

_____

Day Four

> Some trust in chariots and some in horses, but we trust in the name of the Lord our God. (Psalm 20:7, ESV)

Trusting God Yahweh will challenge you to evaluate the way that you view things. You should never place your confidence in material things that can quickly lose their value.

Trusting God In Troubling Times

Focused Prayer

Lord, please help me value what is most important in my life. Help me to understand that I should never place the value of material things over your ability to take care of me. I must learn to place my trust in the reputation of your name as always being a provider. In Jesus, Amen.

My Action Plan

_____

_____

_____

_____

_____

_____

_____

Trusting God In Troubling Times

_____

_____

_____

_____

_____

_____

_____

Personal Blessings I Have Experienced

_____

_____

_____

_____

_____

_____

_____

Trusting God In Troubling Times

Personal Reflection

and

Final Thoughts

Day Five

He changes times and seasons; he removes kings and sets up kings; he gives wisdom to the wise and knowledge to those who have understanding; (Daniel 2:21, ESV)

Times like these require you to trust God Yahweh concerning who is in charge of the United States. Remember that He sets up and He can remove anyone in charge of anything according to His will.

Focused Prayer

> Lord, please give me the peace that I need to trust your divine appointment of the commander and chief of the United States. I need your help to get me to a place where I have comfort in knowing that you are in control at all times. In Jesus' Holy Name, Amen.

My Action Plan

_____

_____

_____

_____

_____

_____

_____

_____

Trusting God In Troubling Times

_____

_____

_____

_____

_____

_____

Personal Blessings I Have Experienced

_____

_____

_____

_____

_____

_____

_____

_____

Trusting God In Troubling Times

Personal Reflection

and

Final Thoughts

_____

_____

_____

_____

_____

_____

_____

_____

_____

_____

_____

_____

_____

Day Six

> For a child will be born to us, a son will be given to us; And the government will rest on His shoulders;... (Isaiah 9:6, LSB)

Trusting God means that you have confidence and assurance in knowing that the world's government is secondary to Jesus Christ's government. He is responsible for the rulership of the world.

Focused Prayer

> Lord, please help me realize that Jesus is the ultimate ruler of this world. I must rest in the fact that I have declared Jesus as my Lord, and He has the responsibility of making sure that I am provided for at all times. Please help me remember this truth. In Christ, Amen.

My Action Plan

_____

_____

_____

_____

_____

_____

_____

_____

Trusting God In Troubling Times

_____

_____

_____

_____

_____

_____

Personal Blessings I Have Experienced

_____

_____

_____

_____

_____

_____

_____

_____

Trusting God In Troubling Times

Personal Reflection

and

Final Thoughts

Day Seven

> I have been young, and now am old, yet I have not seen the righteous forsaken or his children begging for bread. (Psalm 37:25, ESV)

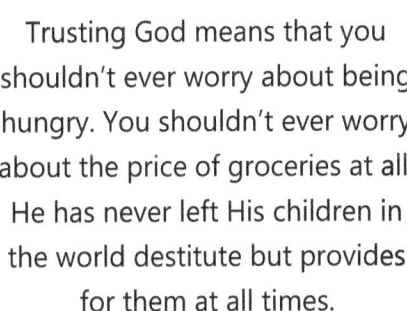

Trusting God means that you shouldn't ever worry about being hungry. You shouldn't ever worry about the price of groceries at all. He has never left His children in the world destitute but provides for them at all times.

Trusting God In Troubling Times

Focused Prayer

> Lord, groceries, especially eggs, are at an all-time high! I need to have a trusting heart, knowing that you will provide for me in spite of the increased cost of feeding my family. Please, Lord, help me have peace knowing that you have my back. Thanks Jesus. Amen.

My Action Plan

_____

_____

_____

_____

_____

_____

_____

_____

Trusting God In Troubling Times

Personal Blessings I Have Experienced

Personal Reflection

and

Final Thoughts

_____

_____

_____

_____

_____

_____

_____

_____

_____

_____

_____

Day Eight

> So Abraham called the name of that place, "The Lord will provide"; as it is said to this day, "On the mount of the Lord it shall be provided. (Genesis 22:14, ESV)

Trusting God means that you shouldn't worry about high gas prices. You must get to the same place Abraham did when he became confident that God would provide all that he needed at the proper time.

Trusting God In Troubling Times

Focused Prayer

> Lord, the price of gas is at an all-time high! I need to have a trusting heart knowing that you will give me the ability to have enough money at all times to put gas in my car in order for me to get to work and arrive home safely. Please Lord, help me have peace in this matter. In Christ, Thanks.

My Action Plan

_____

_____

_____

_____

_____

_____

_____

Trusting God In Troubling Times

_____

_____

_____

_____

_____

Personal Blessings I Have Experienced

_____

_____

_____

_____

_____

_____

_____

_____

Trusting God In Troubling Times

Personal Reflection

and

Final Thoughts

_____

_____

_____

_____

_____

_____

_____

_____

_____

_____

_____

_____

Day Nine

> I have led you forty years in the wilderness. Your clothes have not worn out on you, and your sandals have not worn off your feet.
> (Deuteronomy 29:5, ESV)

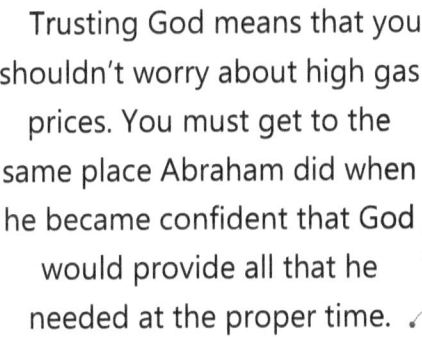

Trusting God means that you shouldn't worry about high gas prices. You must get to the same place Abraham did when he became confident that God would provide all that he needed at the proper time.

Focused Prayer

God Yahweh, I don't want to worry about having clothes on my back and shoes on my feet. Give me the ability to rest in comfort knowing that what you did for your children in the past, you will also do for me. I need your help Lord, concerning this. In Jesus' name, Amen.

My Action Plan

_____

_____

_____

_____

_____

_____

_____

_____

Trusting God In Troubling Times

_____

_____

_____

_____

_____

_____

Personal Blessings I Have Experienced

_____

_____

_____

_____

_____

_____

_____

_____

Trusting God In Troubling Times

Personal Reflection

and

Final Thoughts

Day Ten

> There is neither Jew nor Greek, there is neither slave nor free, there is no male and female, for you are all one in Christ Jesus.
> (Galatians 3:28, ESV)

Trusting God means that you know that you are not viewed differently from anyone else. You must never let anyone devalue the purpose and greatness that He has placed in you to accomplish in your life.

Trusting God In Troubling Times

Focused Prayer

> Yahweh, I need to be reminded by you that I have a right to be treated fairly and not judged based on my racial background. Give me the confidence to stand up for the rights that you gave me when I became a believer! In Jesus' name, Amen.

My Action Plan

_____

_____

_____

_____

_____

_____

_____

Trusting God In Troubling Times

Personal Blessings I Have Experienced

Trusting God In Troubling Times

Personal Reflection

and

Final Thoughts

_____

_____

_____

_____

_____

_____

_____

_____

_____

_____

_____

_____

Day Eleven

"For God shows no partiality.
(Romans 2:11, ESV)

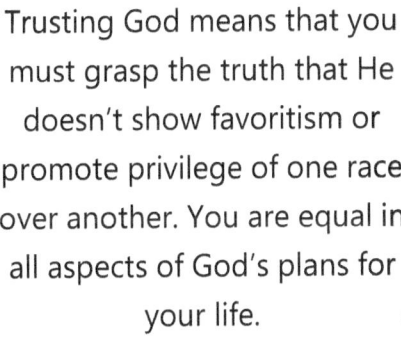

Trusting God means that you must grasp the truth that He doesn't show favoritism or promote privilege of one race over another. You are equal in all aspects of God's plans for your life.

Focused Prayer

> Yahweh, I want to embrace the truth that in your sight I am not inferior or less favored to any other person. Help me become confident in knowing that you have a divine plan for my life that no one can rob me of by talking down to me. In Jesus' name, Amen.

My Action Plan

_____

_____

_____

_____

_____

_____

_____

_____

Trusting God In Troubling Times

_____

_____

_____

_____

_____

_____

Personal Blessings I Have Experienced

_____

_____

_____

_____

_____

_____

_____

_____

Trusting God In Troubling Times

Personal Reflection

and

Final Thoughts

Day Twelve

> O Lord, you hear the desire of the afflicted; you will strengthen their heart; you will incline your ear to do justice to the fatherless and the oppressed, so that man who is of the earth may strike terror no more.
> (Psalm 10:17–18, ESV)

Trusting God means that even though many are oppressing you and causing injustice in your life, you should be encouraged knowing that God Yahweh hears and knows your concerns and will bring justice very soon to you.

Focused Prayer

> Lord, I am viewed and treated unfairly and it is taking a toll on me. I am worn down, and I am losing my confidence. Please assure me that you hear my cry for help and will quickly provide justice for me so that I am treated and viewed fairly. In Jesus' name, Amen.

My Action Plan

_____

_____

_____

_____

_____

_____

_____

_____

_____

Trusting God In Troubling Times

Personal Blessings I Have Experienced

Trusting God In Troubling Times

Personal Reflection

and

Final Thoughts

_____

_____

_____

_____

_____

_____

_____

_____

_____

_____

_____

Day Thirteen

> Unequal weights and unequal measures are both alike an abomination to the Lord.
> (Proverbs 20:10, ESV)

Trusting God means that He is equipping you with the ability to be treated fairly when you do business with others. You shouldn't pay more for a car, house or other goods just because of the color of your skin.

Focused Prayer

> Lord, please move in my heart to have a desire to seek knowledge and learn how to conduct business properly. Help me prepare myself to become knowledgeable about how to buy a house, car and everything else so that that I am never taken advantage of. In Jesus' name, Amen.

My Action Plan

_____

_____

_____

_____

_____

_____

_____

_____

Trusting God In Troubling Times

Personal Blessings I Have Experienced

Trusting God In Troubling Times

Personal Reflection

and

Final Thoughts

_____

_____

_____

_____

_____

_____

_____

_____

_____

_____

_____

Trusting God In Troubling Times

Day Fourteen

> Honor the Lord with your wealth and with the firstfruits of all your produce; then your barns will be filled with plenty, and your vats will be bursting with wine.
> (Proverbs 3:9–10, ESV)

Trusting God means that you must trust Him by giving Him a minimum of ten percent of your gross income. You must show Him that you are putting your money where your praise is.

Trusting God In Troubling Times

Focused Prayer

> Lord, please help me become confident in trusting you with the income you have allowed me to have. Help me realize that I must give back to you that which you have allowed me to earn. I know that all wealth comes from you. I must do the right thing. In Jesus' name, Amen.

My Action Plan

_____

_____

_____

_____

_____

_____

_____

_____

Trusting God In Troubling Times

_____

_____

_____

_____

_____

_____

Personal Blessings I Have Experienced

_____

_____

_____

_____

_____

_____

_____

_____

Trusting God In Troubling Times

Personal Reflection

and

Final Thoughts

Day Fifteen

I will rebuke the devourer for you, so that it will not destroy the fruits of your soil, and your vine in the field shall not fail to bear, says the Lord of hosts. (Malachi 3:11, ESV)

When you trust God, you know that He's always working to protect your hard-earned assets. God Yahweh promises to censure everything that is trying to rob you of what you have.

Focused Prayer

Lord, I am grateful to know that you are always working to censure everything that is trying to rob me of what I have. I also need to be honest and ask you to give me an obedient heart so that I will give at least ten percent back out of all that you have given me. Please help me. In Christ, Amen.

My Action Plan

_____

_____

_____

_____

_____

_____

_____

_____

Trusting God In Troubling Times

_____

_____

_____

_____

_____

Personal Blessings I Have Experienced

_____

_____

_____

_____

_____

_____

_____

_____

Trusting God In Troubling Times

Personal Reflection

and

Final Thoughts

_____

_____

_____

_____

_____

_____

_____

_____

_____

_____

_____

_____

Day Sixteen

> You shall remember the Lord your God, for it is he who gives you power to get wealth, that he may confirm his covenant that he swore to your fathers, as it is this day. (Deuteronomy 8:18, ESV)

Trusting God means that you understand that He and only He gives you the ability and power to get wealthy. You must thank Him for health and strength to be able to make a living.

Focused Prayer

> Lord, I am forever thankful for you giving me health, strength and a sound mind. I know that if I am sick and unable to work, I would not be able to make a living or get in a position to invest my money and become wealthy. I just want to thank you for keeping me healthy Lord. Thank you for giving me the ability to thrive. In Christ, Amen.

My Action Plan

_____

_____

_____

_____

_____

_____

_____

_____

Trusting God In Troubling Times

_____

_____

_____

_____

_____

_____

Personal Blessings I Have Experienced

_____

_____

_____

_____

_____

_____

_____

_____

Trusting God In Troubling Times

Personal Reflection

and

Final Thoughts

Day Seventeen

> "For I know the plans I have for you," declares the Lord, "plans to prosper you and not to harm you, plans to give you hope and a future. (Jeremiah 29:11, NIV84)

You must learn how to trust God Yahweh with your future. He knows your beginning before you begin and He knows your ending before you end. You must ask Him to reveal His divine plan for your life so that you can soar.

Focused Prayer

> Father Yahweh, I am asking you to reveal to me the plans you have for my life. I try and do things my way, but often they never seem to work out right. I need you to guide me into a secure path where I can prosper and grow into all that you have designed me to be. I need your wisdom. I need your love. I need you! In Christ, Amen.

My Action Plan

_____

_____

_____

_____

_____

_____

_____

_____

Trusting God In Troubling Times

Personal Blessings I Have Experienced

Trusting God In Troubling Times

Personal Reflection

and

Final Thoughts

_____

_____

_____

_____

_____

_____

_____

_____

_____

_____

_____

Day Eighteen

And he awoke and rebuked the wind and said to the sea, "Peace! Be still!" And the wind ceased, and there was a great calm. (Mark 4:39, ESV)

Trusting Yahweh means that when it seems like He isn't present during your troublesome experience, He is busy at work preserving your life. You must understand that He operates silently and effectively calms all of your challenges.

Focused Prayer

> Daddy Yahweh, please give me the ability to sense your presence in the midst of my storms. I need to know that you are working things out for me at all times. In Christ's name, Amen.

My Action Plan

_____

_____

_____

_____

_____

_____

_____

_____

Trusting God In Troubling Times

Personal Blessings I Have Experienced

Trusting God In Troubling Times

Personal Reflection

and

Final Thoughts

Day Nineteen

> And the peace of God, which surpasses all understanding, will guard your hearts and your minds in Christ Jesus. (Philippians 4:7, ESV)

The more you trust God Yahweh; the more peace can guard your heart from further hurt and anxiety. Trust puts a wall up between your worries and God's protection and provision.

Focused Prayer

> Daddy Yahweh, please give me the ability to recognize and grasp your peace so that I don't have to obtain and understanding to achieve comfort. I just want to experience your peace in difficult times. In Christ's name, Amen.

My Action Plan

_____

_____

_____

_____

_____

_____

_____

_____

Trusting God In Troubling Times

Personal Blessings I Have Experienced

Trusting God In Troubling Times

Personal Reflection

and

Final Thoughts

Day Twenty

> Do not be anxious about anything, but in everything by prayer and supplication with thanksgiving let your requests be made known to God. (Philippians 4:6, ESV)

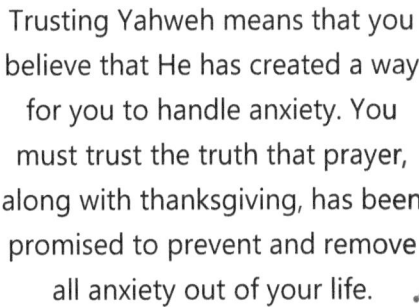

Trusting Yahweh means that you believe that He has created a way for you to handle anxiety. You must trust the truth that prayer, along with thanksgiving, has been promised to prevent and remove all anxiety out of your life.

Focused Prayer

Daddy Yahweh, I'm asking you to give me the ability to place all of my concerns with you. Help me walk in confidence, knowing that prayer is a preventive measure to forgo anxiety and not a reaction to it. IJNA

My Action Plan

_____

_____

_____

_____

_____

_____

_____

_____

Trusting God In Troubling Times

Personal Blessings I Have Experienced

Trusting God In Troubling Times

Personal Reflection

and

Final Thoughts

Day Twenty-One

"Therefore do not be anxious about tomorrow, for tomorrow will be anxious for itself. Sufficient for the day is its own trouble.
(Matthew 6:34, ESV)

Trusting Yahweh means that you shouldn't focus on the challenges and possible failures of the future while missing the blessing of the present day. You must learn to master and maximize the moment that you are in.

Focused Prayer

Daddy Yahweh, help me maximize today and enjoy it. I am tired of missing my blessings because I am too wrapped up in the fear of future failure. Help me see the future success you have for me. In Jesus' name. Amen.

My Action Plan

_____

_____

_____

_____

_____

_____

_____

_____

Trusting God In Troubling Times

Personal Blessings I Have Experienced

Trusting God In Troubling Times

Personal Reflection

and

Final Thoughts

Day Twenty-Two

"I have said these things to you, that in me you may have peace. In the world you will have tribulation. But take heart; I have overcome the world. (John 16:33, ESV)

Trusting Yahweh means that in spite of economic, social, mental and physical adversity, He has given you overcoming power in order to obtain victory and peace when faced with any of these unpleasant occurrences.

Focused Prayer

Daddy Yahweh, I thank you for giving me supernatural power to overcome any economic, social, mental or physical challenge that I might face. I am so grateful to have your anointing. In Jesus' name. Amen.

My Action Plan

_____

_____

_____

_____

_____

_____

_____

_____

Trusting God In Troubling Times

Personal Blessings I Have Experienced

Trusting God In Troubling Times

Personal Reflection

and

Final Thoughts

Day Twenty-Three

> Let the favor of the Lord our God be upon us and establish the work of our hands upon us; yes, establish the work of our hands!
> (Psalm 90:17, ESV)

Trusting Yahweh means that if you are unemployed, have been demoted or even overlooked for a promotion, God has a better plan for your life. He has placed an everlasting gift in your hands to always be able to make a living.

Focused Prayer

> Lord, I thank you for giving me the ability to prosper at all times regardless of my employment status. My hands are anointed and able to prosperously produce at all times. In Jesus' name, Amen.

My Action Plan

_____

_____

_____

_____

_____

_____

_____

_____

Trusting God In Troubling Times

Personal Blessings I Have Experienced

Trusting God In Troubling Times

Personal Reflection

and

Final Thoughts

_____

_____

_____

_____

_____

_____

_____

_____

_____

_____

_____

Day Twenty-Four

> In the morning sow your seed, and at evening withhold not your hand, for you do not know which will prosper, this or that, or whether both alike will be good.
> (Ecclesiastes 11:6, ESV)

Trusting Yahweh means that you should never give up when you become unemployed and you're searching for a new job. You must know that being persistent and confident will produce success for you very soon.

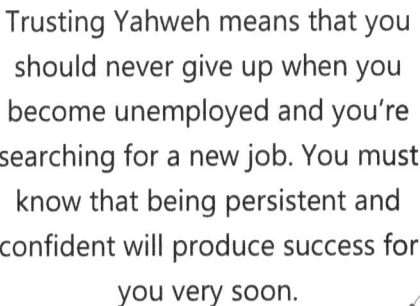

Focused Prayer

Lord, I thank you for giving me a relentless and persistent spirit. I will never quit when challenged with seeking a new career or pursuing a promotion. I know that my success is coming. In Jesus' name Amen.

My Action Plan

_____

_____

_____

_____

_____

_____

_____

_____

_____

Trusting God In Troubling Times

Personal Blessings I Have Experienced

Trusting God In Troubling Times

Personal Reflection

and

Final Thoughts

Day Twenty-Five

> Behold, I am doing a new thing; now it springs forth, do you not perceive it? I will make a way in the wilderness and rivers in the desert. (Isaiah 43:19, ESV)

Trusting Yahweh means that in the dry spell that you are experiencing, He is working on a life-changing transformation for you. Keep your spiritual and physical eyes open to see what He's about to do!

Focused Prayer

Lord, I thank you for giving me the ability to spiritually see your provision for me in what seems like a hopeless and lifeless situation. My eyes are open to receive your blessing. In Christ, Amen.

My Action Plan

_____

_____

_____

_____

_____

_____

_____

_____

Trusting God In Troubling Times

Personal Blessings I Have Experienced

Trusting God In Troubling Times

Personal Reflection

and

Final Thoughts

Day Twenty-Six

> I can do all things through him who strengthens me. (Philippians 4:13, ESV)

Trusting Yahweh means that in good and challenging times, you must have the temperament to be consistent in your attitude toward life and others. You must remain humble and thankful in all of your successes and challenges.

Focused Prayer

> Lord, help me to display a consistent and thankful attitude when you bless me, as well as when I am going through difficult times. I know that the world is watching to see how I react to changes in my life. In Christ, Amen.

My Action Plan

_____

_____

_____

_____

_____

_____

_____

_____

Trusting God In Troubling Times

_____

_____

_____

_____

_____

_____

Personal Blessings I Have Experienced

_____

_____

_____

_____

_____

_____

_____

_____

Trusting God In Troubling Times

Personal Reflection

and

Final Thoughts

Day Twenty-Seven

> The Lord is my shepherd; I shall not want. (Psalm 23:1, ESV)

Yahweh, your shepherd, will provide everything you need if you trust Him. It means that you can expect to receive, at the minimum, your needs to be met and, at the maximum, your deepest heartfelt desires awarded to you.

Focused Prayer

Lord, I thank you for being my personal shepherd. You have been so good to me by always meeting my needs. I also thank you in advance for preparing better things for me as well. You always have the best for me. In Christ, Amen.

My Action Plan

_____

_____

_____

_____

_____

_____

_____

_____

Trusting God In Troubling Times

Personal Blessings I Have Experienced

Trusting God In Troubling Times

Personal Reflection

and

Final Thoughts

Day Twenty-Eight

> And my God will supply every need of yours according to his riches in glory in Christ Jesus. (Philippians 4:19, ESV)

Trusting Yahweh assures you that He always has a ready supply to meet every need that you have. You should never worry about food, clothes, housing, or any other necessity. God Yahweh always has you covered.

Focused Prayer

> Lord, I need you to forgive me for doubting that you weren't concerned about my needs. I know that you are rich in your ability to give me all that I need to enjoy life. In Christ, Amen.

My Action Plan

_____

_____

_____

_____

_____

_____

_____

Trusting God In Troubling Times

_____

_____

_____

_____

_____

_____

_____

Personal Blessings I Have Experienced

_____

_____

_____

_____

_____

_____

_____

Trusting God In Troubling Times

Personal Reflection

and

Final Thoughts

Trusting God In Troubling Times

Day Twenty-Nine

> "And we know that for those who love God all things work together for good, for those who are called according to his purpose. (Romans 8:28, ESV)

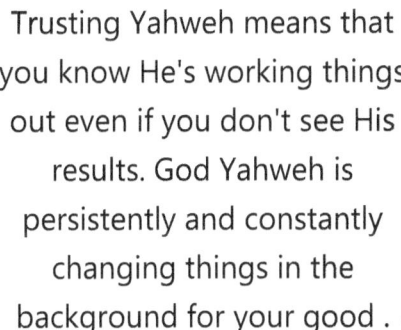

Trusting Yahweh means that you know He's working things out even if you don't see His results. God Yahweh is persistently and constantly changing things in the background for your good .

Trusting God In Troubling Times

Focused Prayer

> Lord, I thank you for not giving up on me during the challenges that I face with anxiety. I know that you constantly work wonders in my life, and I am grateful that you care for my well-being. In Christ, Amen.

My Action Plan

_____

_____

_____

_____

_____

_____

_____

_____

Trusting God In Troubling Times

_____

_____

_____

_____

_____

_____

Personal Blessings I Have Experienced

_____

_____

_____

_____

_____

_____

_____

_____

Trusting God In Troubling Times

Personal Reflection

and

Final Thoughts

Day Thirty

> I sought the Lord, and he answered me and delivered me from all my fears. (Psalm 34:4, ESV)

Trusting Yahweh means that you should never fear anything or anyone. You should know that fear comes to rob you of new opportunities that He has ordained for you to experience in your growth. Fight fear with trust!

Trusting God In Troubling Times

Focused Prayer

> Lord, help me to overcome fear. Help me to see the blessings that you have waiting for me on the other side of every challenge that I face. Thank you for this blessing. In Christ, Amen.

My Action Plan

_____

_____

_____

_____

_____

_____

_____

_____

Trusting God In Troubling Times

_____

_____

_____

_____

_____

_____

Personal Blessings I Have Experienced

_____

_____

_____

_____

_____

_____

_____

_____

Trusting God In Troubling Times

Personal Reflection

and

Final Thoughts

_____

_____

_____

_____

_____

_____

_____

_____

_____

_____

_____

_____

Day Thirty-One

> Count it all joy, my brothers, when you meet trials of various kinds, for you know that the testing of your faith produces steadfastness.
> (James 1:2–3, ESV)

Trusting Yahweh means that you will experience various trials that seem to set you back and rob you of your joy. However, just the opposite is happening. You should be joyful knowing that God Yahweh is advancing you.

Focused Prayer

> Lord, help me to understand that the faster I change my view of trials and welcome them with joy, the faster I will become complete to receive all that you have for me. In Christ, Amen.

My Action Plan

_____

_____

_____

_____

_____

_____

_____

_____

Trusting God In Troubling Times

Personal Blessings I Have Experienced

Trusting God In Troubling Times

Personal Reflection

and

Final Thoughts

_____

_____

_____

_____

_____

_____

_____

_____

_____

_____

_____

_____

Day Thirty-Two

> then the Lord your God will restore your fortunes and have mercy on you,... (Deuteronomy 30:3, ESV)

Trusting Yahweh means that with Him you can never lose anything! If all your possessions have been taken from you, He will show mercy and restore to you everything that you have lost and even give you more than you had before.

Focused Prayer

> Lord, thank you for forgiving me despite my mistakes; that caused me to lose some things. I ask you to help me become a better steward of all that you have given me. In Christ, Amen.

My Action Plan

_____

_____

_____

_____

_____

_____

_____

_____

_____

Trusting God In Troubling Times

Personal Blessings I Have Experienced

Trusting God In Troubling Times

Personal Reflection

and

Final Thoughts

Day Thirty-Three

> Jesus said to her, "I am the resurrection and the life. Whoever believes in me, though he die, yet shall he live, and everyone who lives and believes in me shall never die. Do you believe this?" (John 11:25–26, ESV)

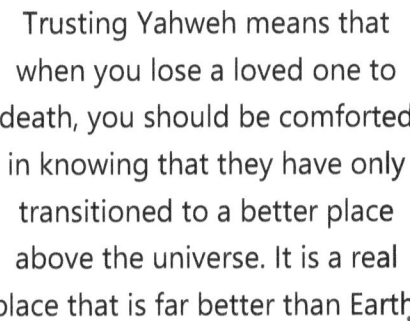

Trusting Yahweh means that when you lose a loved one to death, you should be comforted in knowing that they have only transitioned to a better place above the universe. It is a real place that is far better than Earth.

Focused Prayer

> Lord, help me to find comfort in knowing that the death of a loved one is a new life for them. I must realize that they are experiencing a new reality far better than life here on earth. In Christ, Amen.

My Action Plan

_____

_____

_____

_____

_____

_____

_____

_____

Trusting God In Troubling Times

Personal Blessings I Have Experienced

Trusting God In Troubling Times

Personal Reflection

and

Final Thoughts

_____

_____

_____

_____

_____

_____

_____

_____

_____

_____

_____

_____

Day Thirty-Four

> Yes, we are of good courage, and we would rather be away from the body and at home with the Lord.
> (2 Corinthians 5:8, ESV)

Trusting Yahweh means that you are comforted in knowing that when a loved one dies, they are full of joy because they are in their preferred place. You must know that their choice of residence is to be with the Lord!

Trusting God In Troubling Times

Focused Prayer

Lord, help me to find comfort in knowing that I should be of good courage knowing that my loved one that has passed is abiding in the glory and beauty of the Almighty! In Christ, Amen.

My Action Plan

_____

_____

_____

_____

_____

_____

_____

_____

Trusting God In Troubling Times

Personal Blessings I Have Experienced

Trusting God In Troubling Times

Personal Reflection

and

Final Thoughts

Trusting God In Troubling Times

Day Thirty-Five

"Blessed are those who mourn, for they shall be comforted."
(Matthew 5:4, ESV)

Trusting Yahweh means that as you mourn the loss of a loved one, never forget that He has promised comfort to help you overcome the grief that you are experiencing!

Focused Prayer

> God Yahweh, I thank you for comforting me in my time of loss. I will miss my loved one, but I know that they are in a better place in your arms. I trust all that you do in our lives. In Christ, Amen.

My Action Plan

_____

_____

_____

_____

_____

_____

_____

_____

Trusting God In Troubling Times

_____

_____

_____

_____

_____

_____

Personal Blessings I Have Experienced

_____

_____

_____

_____

_____

_____

_____

_____

Trusting God In Troubling Times

Personal Reflection

and

Final Thoughts

_____

_____

_____

_____

_____

_____

_____

_____

_____

_____

_____

Day Thirty-Six

> But the centurion replied, "Lord, I am not worthy to have you come under my roof, but only say the word, and my servant will be healed." (Matthew 8:8, ESV)

Trusting Yahweh means that you are confident that a spoken word sent from heaven will have a healing effect on you. Nothing can separate you from a healing word sent from on high.

Focused Prayer

God Yahweh, help me to have faith to know that when you speak a word of healing directly to me, it will be effective in my life with whatever illness I have. In Christ, Amen.

My Action Plan

_____

_____

_____

_____

_____

_____

_____

_____

_____

_____

_____

Trusting God In Troubling Times

_____

_____

_____

_____

_____

_____

Personal Blessings I Have Experienced

_____

_____

_____

_____

_____

_____

_____

Trusting God In Troubling Times

Personal Reflection

and

Final Thoughts

Day Thirty-Seven

> That evening they brought to him many who were oppressed by demons, and he cast out the spirits with a word and healed all who were sick. (Matthew 8:16,

Trusting Yahweh means that you know that Christ can heal anyone at any time according to the will of God Yahweh! You must never doubt His ability to heal you when you are not feeling well.

Trusting God In Troubling Times

Focused Prayer

> God Yahweh, I believe that you can heal me of all illnesses that I might experience. I have faith to trust that your will is always done in accordance with your divine plan for my life. In Christ, Amen.

My Action Plan

_____

_____

_____

_____

_____

_____

_____

_____

Trusting God In Troubling Times

_____

_____

_____

_____

_____

_____

Personal Blessings I Have Experienced

_____

_____

_____

_____

_____

_____

_____

_____

Trusting God In Troubling Times

Personal Reflection

and

Final Thoughts

_____

_____

_____

_____

_____

_____

_____

_____

_____

_____

_____

_____

Day Thirty-Eight

Is anyone among you sick? Let him call for the elders of the church, and let them pray over him, anointing him with oil in the name of the Lord. ...(James 5:14–15, ESV)

Trusting Yahweh means that you have no problem going to elders and anointed believers in your church and telling them what you are dealing with in addition to allowing them to pray for your wellness.

Trusting God In Troubling Times

Focused Prayer

God Yahweh, thank you for providing elders and anointed leaders in my life that have been given the gift of healing for those of us who may be battling with an illness. In Christ, Amen.

My Action Plan

_____

_____

_____

_____

_____

_____

_____

_____

_____

_____

Trusting God In Troubling Times

Personal Blessings I Have Experienced

Trusting God In Troubling Times

Personal Reflection

and

Final Thoughts

Day Thirty-Nine

> It is in vain that you rise up early and go late to rest, eating the bread of anxious toil; for he gives to his beloved sleep. (Psalm 127:2, ESV)

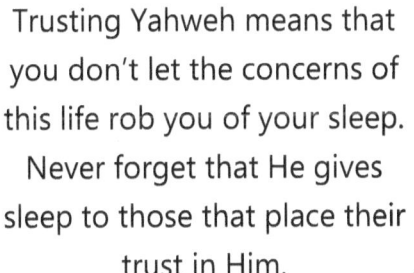

Trusting Yahweh means that you don't let the concerns of this life rob you of your sleep. Never forget that He gives sleep to those that place their trust in Him.

Focused Prayer

God Yahweh, please allow me to release my anxieties to you and not be concerned with things I have no control over. I want to have a restful night of sleep that can only come from you. I thank you for this. In Christ, Amen.

My Action Plan

_____

_____

_____

_____

_____

_____

_____

_____

Trusting God In Troubling Times

Personal Blessings I Have Experienced

Trusting God In Troubling Times

Personal Reflection

and

Final Thoughts

Day Forty

> If you lie down, you will not be afraid; when you lie down, your sleep will be sweet. (Proverbs 3:24, ESV)

Trusting Yahweh means that you can rest assured that fear, doubt and anxiety will not rob you of a good night's sleep. In fact, He promises to make sure that your sleep is peaceful.

Focused Prayer

God Yahweh, I am asking you to give me the ability to place all of my concerns on you so that I can get a good night's sleep. I really want to be able to rest and be refreshed. In Christ, Amen.

My Action Plan

_____

_____

_____

_____

_____

_____

_____

_____

Trusting God In Troubling Times

Personal Blessings I Have Experienced

Trusting God In Troubling Times

Personal Reflection

and

Final Thoughts

_____

_____

_____

_____

_____

_____

_____

_____

_____

_____

_____

_____

Trusting God In Troubling Times

Day Forty-One

> In peace I will both lie down and sleep; for you alone, O Lord, make me dwell in safety. (Psalm 4:8, ESV)

Trusting Yahweh means that you should not let fear disrupt your ability to get a good night's rest. You must know that He watches over you and your concerns twenty-four hours a day!

Trusting God In Troubling Times

Focused Prayer

> God Yahweh, please give me the ability to know that I am safe in your care as you provide for me in all areas of my life. I should never be afraid of anything at all concerning my life. In Christ, Amen.

My Action Plan

_____

_____

_____

_____

_____

_____

_____

_____

Trusting God In Troubling Times

Personal Blessings I Have Experienced

Trusting God In Troubling Times

Personal Reflection

and

Final Thoughts

Day Forty-Two

> Finally, brothers, whatever is true, whatever is honorable, whatever is just, whatever is pure, whatever is lovely, whatever is commendable, if there is any excellence, if there is anything worthy of praise, think about these things. (Philippians 4:8, ESV)

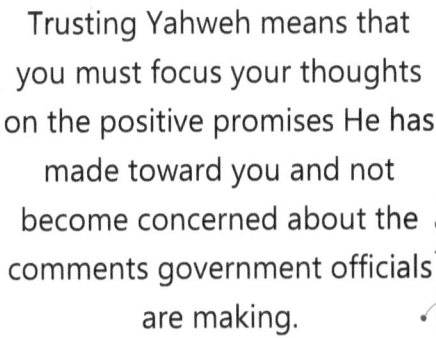

Trusting Yahweh means that you must focus your thoughts on the positive promises He has made toward you and not become concerned about the comments government officials are making.

Focused Prayer

God Yahweh, please give me the ability to block all the negativity that is taking place in our government and the leadership of our country. Help me focus on your promises spoken to me. In Christ, Amen.

My Action Plan

_____

_____

_____

_____

_____

_____

_____

_____

Trusting God In Troubling Times

_____

_____

_____

_____

_____

_____

Personal Blessings I Have Experienced

_____

_____

_____

_____

_____

_____

_____

Trusting God In Troubling Times

Personal Reflection

and

Final Thoughts

_____

_____

_____

_____

_____

_____

_____

_____

_____

_____

_____

_____

Day Forty-Three

> But avoid irreverent babble, for it will lead people into more and more ungodliness, (2 Timothy 2:16, ESV)

Trusting Yahweh means that you know how to ignore comments that are not building you up. You must learn how to tune out negative chatter in order for positive blessings to flow to you.

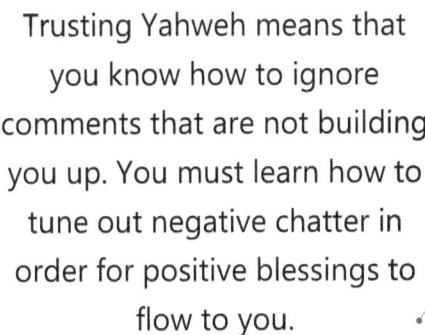

Focused Prayer

> Lord, grant me the ability to concentrate on the promises you reveal to me through the reading of your word and fervent prayer. I trust your word for peace and prosperity. In Christ, Amen.

My Action Plan

_____

_____

_____

_____

_____

_____

_____

_____

_____

Trusting God In Troubling Times

Personal Blessings I Have Experienced

Personal Reflection

and

Final Thoughts

_____

_____

_____

_____

_____

_____

_____

_____

_____

_____

_____

Day Forty-Four

> First of all, then, I urge that supplications, prayers, intercessions, and thanksgivings be made for all people, for kings and all who are in high positions, that we may lead a peaceful and quiet life, godly and dignified in every way. (1 Timothy 2:1–2, ESV)

You must pray daily for all those in authority over your life if you trust Yahweh. You know that only prayer being lifted up daily for the leaders of our country can bring peace and equity on this earth for all mankind.

Trusting God In Troubling Times

Focused Prayer

> Lord, please place in my heart an insatiable desire to pray for the leader of our country daily. Help him use wisdom under your direction in all decisions that are being made. In Christ, Amen.

My Action Plan

_____

_____

_____

_____

_____

_____

_____

_____

Personal Blessings I Have Experienced

Trusting God In Troubling Times

Personal Reflection

and

Final Thoughts

Day Forty-Five

> For kingship belongs to the Lord, and he rules over the nations. (Psalm 22:28, ESV)

Trusting Yahweh means that every living person's well-being in this country is in His hands. Nothing can happen without Him allowing it to take place, as He is in control. He is the ruler over everything on this earth!

Trusting God In Troubling Times

Focused Prayer

Lord, I surrender all of my fear, doubt and mistrust of our governmental leaders into your hand. I know that you protect and provide for your children. I rest in this confidently. In Christ, Amen.

My Action Plan

_____

_____

_____

_____

_____

_____

_____

_____

Trusting God In Troubling Times

Personal Blessings I Have Experienced

Trusting God In Troubling Times

Personal Reflection

and

Final Thoughts

Day Forty-Six

> Let every person be subject to the governing authorities. For there is no authority except from God, and those that exist have been instituted by God. (Romans 13:1, ESV)

When you trust Yahweh, you can feel secure in the knowledge that He holds the ultimate authority over our government in this country. God Yahweh is a just and equitable God, and His rulership will always reign throughout this earth.

Focused Prayer

> Lord, I must realize that you are in control of this government. Help me understand that what we are seeing in this country has been allowed by you for your purpose. Everything is and will be well in the end. In Christ, Amen.

My Action Plan

_____

_____

_____

_____

_____

_____

_____

_____

Trusting God In Troubling Times

_____

_____

_____

_____

_____

_____

Personal Blessings I Have Experienced

_____

_____

_____

_____

_____

_____

_____

_____

Trusting God In Troubling Times

Personal Reflection

and

Final Thoughts

Day Forty-Seven

> And Jesus came and said to them, "All authority in heaven and on earth has been given to me. (Matthew 28:18, ESV)

Trusting Yahweh means that you can celebrate the truth that Jesus Christ is King and ruler with all authority in His hand. He is a great, just and faithful ruler. You must stay patient and let Him work everything out for the good of this country.

Focused Prayer

> Lord, I thank you for growing my trust in you, knowing that you are the ultimate authority on this earth. No kingdom on this earth is greater than yours. Thanks for being my king. In Christ, Amen.

My Action Plan

_____

_____

_____

_____

_____

_____

_____

_____

_____

Trusting God In Troubling Times

_____

_____

_____

_____

_____

_____

Personal Blessings I Have Experienced

_____

_____

_____

_____

_____

_____

_____

_____

Trusting God In Troubling Times

Personal Reflection

and

Final Thoughts

_____

_____

_____

_____

_____

_____

_____

_____

_____

_____

_____

_____

Epilogue

One of the best ways to experience God's trust at new levels in your life is for you to give your life to Christ Jesus. Repeat these simple words, and it will become a reality. Repeat the following: Lord Christ Jesus, as of this very moment, I accept you as Lord and Savior of my life. I now give my life to you so it can be fashioned for your purpose and glory. God, I believe everything I've said and confessed to you. I know now that I have received everlasting life based on the work that Christ has done and will continue to do in my life. Jesus, thank you for bringing me to this point where I surrender everything to you. It is in the Holy Spirit through Christ Jesus; I say Amen.

Humbly Yours in Christ

Apostle Jamie T. Pleasant

Epilogue

Book Dr. Jamie Pleasant for a Speaking Engagement!

For speaking engagements, please contact Dr. Jamie T. Pleasant at admin@newzionchristianchurch.org or 678.845.7055

About the Author

Apostle Jamie T. Pleasant, Ph.D., a modern-day polymath, is the founder and Chief Executive Pastor of New Zion Christian Church in Suwanee, Georgia. He currently serves as a tenured Full Professor of Marketing at Clark Atlanta University's School of Business. Notably, he is the first faculty member in the university's history to be accepted into Mensa International, the world's largest and oldest high IQ society for individuals who have scored in the 98th percentile or above on an intelligence test.

Dr. Pleasant is the first African American to graduate from the Georgia Institute of Technology (Georgia Tech) with a Ph.D. in Business Management with a concentration in Marketing, earning that degree in August 1999. He is a 2016 recipient of the "Lifetime Achievement Award" from former President Barack Obama of the USA for volunteer and community service. He was awarded the "Game Changer" Educator Award by

About the Author

Reverend Jesse Jackson at the 2019 Rainbow PUSH International Convention. As a polyhistor, in addition to obtaining a doctorate degree in Business Management from the Georgia Institute of Technology, he holds a bachelor's degree in physics from Benedict College in Columbia, South Carolina, Marketing Studies from Clemson University and an M.B.A. in Marketing from the very prestigious, Clark Atlanta University.

Under his leadership, New Zion has grown from three members when it started in 1995 to well over 700 in weekly attendance, with a focus on economic and entrepreneurial development. God gave him the vision to establish a Biblically based economic development initiative for New Zion Christian Church. He remains at the pulse of the economic business sector in American society.

As a result, Apostle Pleasant is in constant demand to train, speak and teach others at all levels in ministry and the private sector about business and economic development across the country. He has created numerous cutting edge and industry leading

About the Author

ministerial, business and economic development classes and programs, along with SAT & PSAT prep courses for children ages 9-19. He founded The Financial Literacy Academy for Youth (FLAFY), where youth between the ages of 13-19 attend 12-week intense classes on financial money management principles. At the end of those 12 weeks, they receive a "Personal Finance" certificate of achievement. In 2015, he established The Young Leadership and Success Academy that teaches young people between the ages of 10-21 how to invest, make presentations and start and operate businesses. Other ministries he has pioneered include The Wealth Builders Investment Club (WBIC), which educates and allows members to actively invest in the stock market, along with the much-celebrated Institute of Entrepreneurship (IOE), where participants earn a certificate in entrepreneurship after three months of comprehensive training in all aspects of starting and owning a successful competitive business. The main goal and purpose of IOE is that each year one of the trained businesses will be awarded up to $10,000 startup money to ensure financial success.

About the Author

Apostle Pleasant has met with political officials such as former President Bill Clinton and Nelson Mandela. He has performed marriage ceremonies and counseled numerous celebrated personalities such as Usher Raymond, Terri Vaughn, and many others. Several gospel music artists have performed at the church, including Tiff Joy. Each year, Apostle Pleasant conducts chapel services for Clemson University's football team and is a spiritual and personal friend to its two-time national championship head coach, Dabo Swinney.

As a modern-day civil rights leader, he is a close aide to Reverend Jesse Jackson and serves on the Board of Directors of Rainbow PUSH Inc. (Atlanta) and Director of Business Education and Corporate Engagement. He serves on the Board of Fellowship of Christian Athletes (Atlanta Urban) and after the Columbine High School shooting, he founded the National School Safety Advocacy Association. His latest foundations include the Young Entrepreneurship Program (YEP) and the African American Consumer Economic Rights (AACER).

About the Author

He has authored numerous books that include: *Prayer Changes Things, Powerful Prayers That Open Heaven, Capturing and Keeping the Pastor's Heart, Unshakable Faith, Proverbs for Prosperity, How to release Your Blessings Through Service in Ministry, When Purpose is at Work, Today's Apostles (2024 ed.), Advertising Principles: How to Effectively Reach African Americans in the 21st Century, Discover a New You: A 21 Day Journey to Uncovering Your Uniqueness, Daily Quotes for Daily Blessings, The Making of a Man, I'm Just Sayin', From My Heart To Yours: Love Letters From A Loving Father, Today's Apostle: Servants of God Leading His People towards Unity, A 7 Day Prayer Plan for Prosperity, You Have What It Takes, A Marketing Model for Ethnic Consumer Behavior, An Overview of Strategic Healthcare Marketing and The Importance of Subcultural Marketing.*

Apostle Pleasant is a lifetime member of Alpha Phi Alpha Fraternity Inc. He is the loving husband of the pulchritudinous Kimberly Pleasant and the proud father of three children: Christian, Zion and Nacara.

About the Author

About the Author

FINI

About the Author

About the Author

About the Author

www.ingramcontent.com/pod-product-compliance
Lightning Source LLC
Chambersburg PA
CBHW022007160426
43197CB00007B/316